W9-DAV-468

MESOPOTAMIA INVENTING OUR WORLD

CLEMENS REICHEL

Special thanks to Sarah Collins, curator of *Mesopotamia*,
for her descriptions of the British Museum artifacts

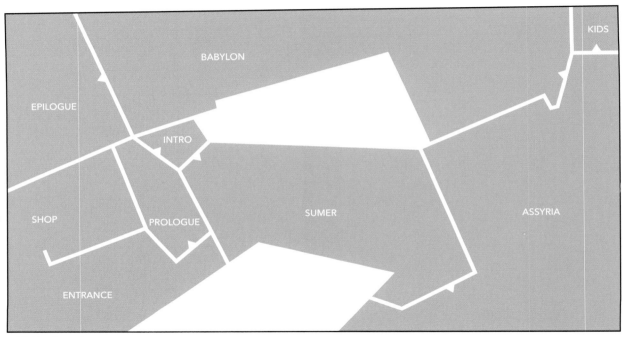

exhibition floor plan

CONTENTS

FOREWORD

t's difficult not to think of the phrase the *cradle of civilization* when you see the remarkable artifacts in the Mesopotamia exhibition. These objects speak to a moment in history where many elements of civilization, as we know it today, took form. They also represent the enduring presence of this ancient time in our world now. Our life today is informed by the innovations of Mesopotamia—a theme we are emphasising in our presentation of the British Museum's landmark exhibition. We are encouraging our visitors to understand the accomplishments and struggles of Mesopotamia as relevant today, and as giving insight into contemporary themes imperative to us.

We are grateful to our colleagues at the British Museum for allowing this show to come to Toronto and, in fact, make its only North American stop here. The ROM values our relationships with the great museums of the world, such as the British Museum, and our ability to collaborate with them makes exhibitions like Mesopotamia possible for our audiences.

Our new visual identity suggests the "O" of the ROM as a lens into the Museum's collections and research, and that the ROM gives access to information about the natural and cultural worlds. With an exhibition such as Mesopotamia, the "O" is also a portal into the world's great institutions and their extraordinary collections that the ROM can present to our visitors.

Janet Carding
Director & CEO
Royal Ontario Museum

INTRODUCTION

Set in a landscape that is defined by the rivers Tigris and Euphrates, Mesopotamia (the area of present-day Iraq) was home to many of humanity's great social and technological achievements: Home to the Agricultural Revolution and the domestication of animals, it gave rise to the first villages, cities, and empires. It also saw the invention of writing, the establishment of codified law, and the first recordings of mathematical equations and astronomical observation. Many of these great inventions continue to shape our lives today. This summer, the ROM will bring the fascinating worlds of ancient Sumer, Assyria, and Babylonia to Toronto. *Mesopotamia: Inventing Our World*, a British Museum exhibition presented in collaboration with the ROM, provides deep insights into this mysterious world that has significantly impacted our present day lives.

The exhibition features more than 170 objects from the British Museum's collection, as well as numerous iconic artifacts from well-known North American collections: the University of Pennsylvania Museum of Archaeology and Anthropology (Penn Museum, Philadelphia), the University of Chicago's Oriental Institute Museum, the Detroit Institute of Arts, and the ROM's own collection. Many of these artifacts were recovered during major excavations undertaken in Iraq during the 19th and 20th century, and hence can be directly connected to the story of some of Mesopotamia's most famous cities—names that may be familiar to audiences from the Biblical tradition.

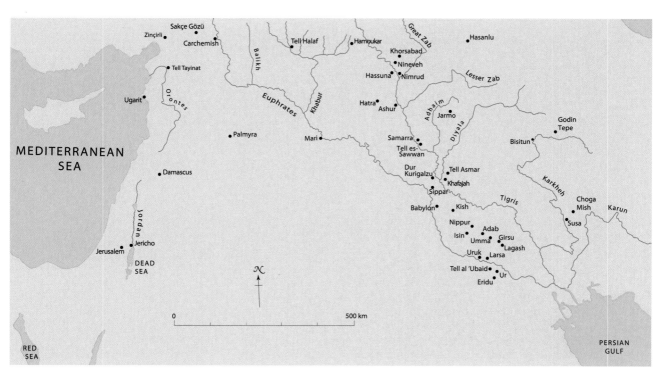

Map of Mesopotamia and surrounding regions, showing sites mentioned in the text.

The city of Ur is highlighted through finds from the Royal Cemetery—magnificent gold vessels and jewelry, a large musical lyre decorated with previous inlays, and a delicate figure of a rearing goat (often called "Ram in a Thicket"). World-famous reliefs from the Assyrian capital of Nimrud and Nineveh feature violent battle scenes and dramatic lion hunts. The history of Babylon is highlighted through artifacts that reflect two of the city's most famous kings: Hammurapi, the great law-giver, and Nebuchadnezzar, conqueror of Jerusalem, who led its inhabitants into exile ("Babylonian Captivity") but also built some of Babylon's most famous monuments, including the ziqqurat (the biblical "Tower of Babel") and the Ishtar Gate.

The first section of this guidebook presents descriptions and photographs of those artifacts that represent the visual and topical highlights of the exhibition. In addition to the aforementioned "Ram caught in a Thicket" these also include a carefully modeled alabaster statue of the Assyrian king Ashurnasirpal II (883–858 BC), and a terracotta relief of a striding lion from the palace of king Nebuchadnezzar in Babylon. This section is followed by a narrative summary of Mesopotamian prehistory and history between 10,000 and 300 BC. Following an introduction to Mesopotamia's landscape and the history of excavations in this area, a longer summary on Mesopotamia's prehistory, describes the Neolithic and Chalcolithic cultures that set the stage for the great civilizations of Mesopotamia highlighted in the exhibit. The narrative in this section is divided by distinct chronological periods. Within each section, specific topics, inventions, or achievements are highlighted. By focusing on the ROM's own Mesopotamian artifact collection for illustrations, we hope that this summary will continue to serve as an introduction to our own Middle Eastern exhibit in the Wirth Gallery of the Middle East, and hence be of lasting value beyond the exhibit period of *Mesopotamia: Inventing Our World*.

Clemens Reichel
Associate Curator, Ancient Near East
Royal Ontario Museum

EXHIBITION HIGHLIGHTS

EARLY ADMINISTRATIVE TABLET

Clay
3300–3000 BC
Probably from Uruk
H: 8.5 cm; W: 7 cm; D: 2 cm
BM 140854

This administrative tablet is written in an early archaic, 'proto-cuneiform' script that is not yet fully understood. It is a list of large quantities of barley allocated to officials and men with civic responsibilities, who are ranked in order of the importance of their profession. Five different types of numerical symbols, formed by deeply impressed shapes including circles and semi-circles, represent the quantities. A stalk of barley is drawn on the reverse of the tablet to show the commodity being quantified and next to this are two signs that can be read as *Ku* and *Shim*. Kushim is mentioned in other texts of this time and is probably the name of the administrator allocating the barley. Kushim seems to have been responsible for a storage facility containing malt and barley, the basic ingredients for the production of beer.

CYLINDER SEAL: PRESENTATION SCENE

Calcite
2100-2000 BC
Provenance unknown
H: 2.54 cm; D: 1.58 cm
BM 132848

Presentation scenes generally show a worshipper being led by a god or goddess towards another deity who is usually seated. Occasionally such scenes show a king in place of the seated deity. On this cylinder seal a shaven-headed worshipper wearing a fringed robe and raising his right hand as a respectful greeting, is being led by his left hand by a goddess towards the water god who is sitting on a throne. The deities are indicated by their horned headdresses and the water god is holding a vase from which flow two streams of water. The inscription states that this seal belonged to *Girsu-ki-du, servant of Mushni the chief of sculptors.*

VOTIVE STATUE OF A SUMERIAN WOMAN

Limestone
c. 2500 BC
From Lagash
H: 34 cm; W: 15.8 cm; D: 13.5 cm
BM 90929

The Sumerians placed stone statues of themselves in temples to represent their presence before the gods. These votive statues of men and women are of various sizes with different hairstyles and costumes but they generally stand or sit with hands respectfully clasped as if in constant prayer. The deep eye sockets were originally inlaid with materials such as shell, lapis lazuli and steatite to make the eyes appear more life-like. The feet are usually shown in relief rather than being carved in the round. This woman's feet are in low relief and the back of her clothing is not defined but the details of her toes, features, and hair are carefully depicted. She wears her garment wrapped over her left shoulder which is a style worn by both men and women. Many statues are anonymous but some that were commissioned by important people are inscribed with their names.

MOSAIC COLUMN DRUM

Shell, pink limestone, and black shale
c. 2500 BC
From Tell al-'Ubaid, Ninhursag Temple
H: 59 cm; Diam: 31 cm
BM 115328

This is one section from a column that decorated the temple
of Ninhursag, the Sumerian mother goddess. Several columns
were found, measuring up to 3.30 metres tall, and they may
have been set on either side of the temple entrance. Originally
the columns had a core of palm logs covered with bitumen, a
naturally occurring tar-like substance that was readily available
in Mesopotamia. Rings of copper wire were attached to the back
of the mosaic inlay pieces of mother-of-pearl, pink limestone
and black shale, and the wire rings were stuck into the bitumen
to hold the inlays in place.

FOUNDATION FIGURINE

Copper alloy
2094–2047 BC
From Ur
H: 23.5 cm; W: 6.98 cm; D: 4 cm
BM 118605

This foundation figure was found together with a steatite tablet in the temple of the goddess Nimintaba at Ur, and dates to the reign of King Shulgi (2094–2047 BC). This is typical of foundation pegs of this period and shows the king in the act of carrying a 'sacred basket' of building materials on his head. Sacred baskets are mentioned in contemporary cuneiform documents regarding the foundation of temples. Although the practice of depositing figurines in foundations was eventually discontinued, they were preserved in the temple foundation boxes. These were sometimes opened and then the figurines would be anointed and ritually reburied for future kings to discover. The image of the king personally taking part in the construction of a temple by carrying a basket on his head continued to be a significant symbol of kingly piety for many centuries. A stone monument in the exhibition , dating to 668–655 BC, depicts King Ashurbanipal in the very same pose. (page 31).

VOTIVE STATUE OF MALE WORSHIPPER

Alabaster
2650–2550 BC (Early Dynastic II)
From Khafaje, Nintu Temple V
H: 30 cm; W: 12.9 cm; Th: 12.4 cm
UM 37-15-31 (Kh. VIII 272)

This alabaster statue, one of the best preserved examples of Early Dynastic votive sculpture, represents a bare-chested, bald-headed male whose hands are folded, angled slightly upwards towards the chest. He is wearing a skirt composed of tiers of tufts (rendered in a fashion similar to animal fleece, though the material intended to be shown here remains uncertain). His eyes are inlaid with shell and lapis lazuli. Although the figure's stature is squat and stocky, its features are rounder and smoother than most contemporary pieces, which are square and blocky. The appearance of bald-headed, clean-shaven statues, often alongside long-haired, bearded male figures, is notable, but it remains unclear whether those are meant to identify different groups among the worshippers or simply represent different stylistic conventions.

DRINKING CUP

Gold
c. 2500 BC
From The Queen's Grave (PG 800)
H: 14 cm; W: 18 cm; D: 12 cm
BM 121346

This was found together with other gold vessels among the many grave goods deposited in the death pit in Queen Puabi's grave. Gold vessels dating to the Early Dynastic Period have so far been discovered only in the Royal Cemetery at Ur. Gold was beaten into thin sheets and vessels formed either from a single sheet or from separate pieces attached together by heating or soldering. The surface decoration was achieved by chasing.

This fluted cup is biconvex in shape and has a long spout that curves upwards. Since it could not have been for pouring, the spout must have been used like a straw. Long straws are illustrated in ceremonial banquet scenes and drinking tubes of silver and gold have been found in some of the Royal Tombs. It is likely that these were used for drinking beer as it contained sediment or particles that needed to be filtered out.

HEADDRESS WITH GOLD LEAVES

Gold, lapis lazuli, and carnelian
c. 2500 BC
From the King's Grave (PG 789)
L: 39.5 cm; leaves L: 5.3 cm (av.)
BM 121483

The majority of the attendants found in the death pits of the
tombs were women. Most of them wore a similar selection of
elaborate headdress, necklaces, and earrings; their clothing,
which did not survive, was also decorated with beads. This
headdress was worn by one of the many female attendants of an
unnamed man whose tomb is known as the 'King's Grave.' It is
composed of carnelian and lapis lazuli beads with gold pendants
in the shape of leaves. Plants—especially leaves, fruits, and
floral rosettes—were popular motifs in Sumerian jewellery. The
delicate leaves would have hung down above the eyebrows of the
wearer. Headdresses of this type are generally not long enough to
encircle the head so they may have been attached to the hair or
the ends were tied with string. Sometimes several were worn in
layers, one above the other.

REARING GOAT WITH A FLOWERING PLANT

Gold, silver, lapis lazuli, shell, copper
2550–2400 BC (Early Dynastic IIIa)
From Ur, Royal Cemetery (grave PG 1237)
H: 42 cm; W: 27 cm; Th: 18 cm
UM 30-12-702 (U.12357)

This sculpture of a goat rearing upright, frequently referred to as "Ram Caught in a Thicket" (an anachronistic reference to the Biblical Abraham/Isaac story) is one of two in the "Great Death Pit" (PG1237) at Ur's Royal Cemetery. Made of numerous precious materials its appearance was colourful and striking. The fleece was made of shell pieces and lapis lazuli, while the face and feet were modelled in gold sheets. The ears were made of copper and the horns of lapis lazuli, while the underbelly was made of silver. The highly stylized plant, composed of several leaves and plants, was wrapped in gold sheets.

Not intended to be a free-standing sculpture, it was most likely the base for a small table top or incense burner, as indicated in similar depictions on contemporary cylinder seals.

GREAT LYRE

Gold, lapis lazuli, shell, bitumen
2550-2400 BC, Early Dynastic IIIa
From the Royal Cemetary (grave PG 789)
W: 140 cm (max.); H: 117 cm (max.)
Bull's head: 40 x 25 x 19 cm
Panel: 31.5 x 11 x 1.5 cm
B17694 (U.10556)

The wooden frame of this lyre, the largest one from the Royal
Cemetery, had perished, but its shape was preserved through
an impression in the soil, allowing for a full reconstruction.
Shaped like an irregular trapezoid, it consists of two uprights
and a sound box. Its front part was decorated with a large bull's
head covered in gold sheet, its large beard made of a single piece
of lapis lazuli. Below it, a front panel inlaid with shell pieces in
bitumen shows four scenes:
- a nude male ("hero" figure) mastering two human-headed bulls
- a lion and hyena bringing food and drink for a banquet
- a musical scene with a donkey playing a bull-headed lyre, a
dancing bear, and a fox playing a sistrum
- a gazelle with two tumblers accompanied by a scorpion man.
    Similar animal banquets are shown in Early Dynastic glyptic
art. Their exact connotation remains uncertain, but it is likely to
have been humorous.

STANDING STATUE OF GUDEA

Paragonite
c. 2100 BC, Lagash II Dynasty
Purchased (most likely from Girsu)
H: 41 cm
F82.5 (82.64)

Gudea, a ruler of the state of Lagash, commissioned numerous
statues of himself in either standing or sitting position. These
statues, which were mostly found at Lagash's capital city of
Girsu, bear inscriptions that each honour a specific god, often
commemorating temple constructions or gifts. The present
statue, dedicated to Geštinanna, wife of Gudea's personal
god Ningišzida, is unusual since it combines elements from
"canonical" Gudea sculpture—a wrapped garment with bare
right shoulder and a brimmed cap—with stylistic elements that
remind of royal sculpture from the earlier Akkadian Period.
Such elements include a very naturalistic rendering of garment
wrinkles, the modelling and position of his hands, but also a
dynamic body posture that seems to indicate movement. Some
scholars have seen the youthful rendering of Gudea's face as
indication that this statue was fashioned early in his reign—
predating the more static demeanor that dominates most of his
statuary—but too little is known about the internal chronology
of Gudea's statues to ascertain this.

STATUE OF KING ASHURNASIRPAL II

Magnesite (statue), red limestone (base)
875–860 BC
From Nimrud, Temple of Ishtar Sharrat-niphi
Statue H: 113 cm; W: 32 cm: D: 15 cm. Base H: 77.5 cm; W: 56.5 cm; D: 37 cm
BM 118871

This is a rare surviving example of an Assyrian sculpture in the round. It was placed on the base on which it stands in a temple at Nimrud (ancient Kalhu). The types of hard stone used for the statue and base are both unusual but it had become common practice for Mesopotamian kings to obtain exotic stone for their votive statues.

King Ashurnasirpal is wearing a fringed shawl wrapped around his body and secured with a belt. In his left hand he holds the mace of authority and in his right hand he carries a ceremonial sickle-sword of a type that gods used to fight monsters. The inscription carved on his chest proclaims his titles and lineage, and ends with the words *king of the universe, king of Assyria, conqueror from the opposite bank of the Tigris as far as Mount Lebanon and the Great Sea, all lands from east to west he*

EAGLE-HEADED SPIRIT AND SACRED TREE

Gypsum
c. 875–860 BC
From Nimrud, North West Palace
H: 141 cm; W: 95 cm; D: 4 cm
BM 102487

Magical spirits and symbolic trees were placed in doorways and throne rooms of Assyrian palaces to ensure protection for the king and palace. This wall relief shows a winged eagle-headed spirit. He holds a cone, described in Assyrian texts as a purifier, which was used to sprinkle liquid from the bucket he carries in his left hand. It is thought the cone and bucket are based on a traditional technique for fertilizing date palms.

On the right is half of a Sacred Tree, a symbol of great importance in Assyria that probably represented the fertility or abundance of the land.

Above the scene is part of a text that lists King Ashurnasirpal's numerous conquests and describes how he built the city of Nimrud. He also refers to these protective wall reliefs:

I made beasts of mountain and seas in white limestone and alabaster and stationed them at the doors.

WOMAN AT THE WINDOW

Ivory
9th–8th century BC
From Nimrud, North West Palace
H: 11 cm; W: 8.85 cm; D: 1.4 cm
BM 118159

Chairs, tables, beds, and elaborate boxes used in the Assyrian palaces were decorated with delicate plaques of carved elephant ivory. The wooden structures to which they were attached have not survived but large quantities of these ivory carvings have been discovered in Assyria, mainly during excavations at Nimrud. Ivory carving was a particular speciality of Phoenician craftsmen of Lebanon who were heavily influenced by Egyptian motifs and designs. Many ivories found in Nimrud originated in Phoenicia but there were also ivory-carving centres in Syria and some ivories may have been produced in Assyria. This plaque shows a woman with an Egyptian hairstyle looking out a window over a window-sill supported by palm columns. At the top and bottom of the scene there are tenons for attachment and on the back a Phoenician or West Semitic letter 'g' is incised twice, probably to indicate where it is to be fixed on the item of furniture.

PANEL SHOWING BEARDED MALE, FACING RIGHT

Ivory
Late 8th century BC, Neo-Assyrian
from Nimrud, Fort Shalmaneser room SW 7
H: 28.5 cm; W: 10 cm; D: 0.9 cm
ROM 959.91.3 (ND 7913)

This panel, one of a set of four, depicts a bearded male figure facing right, standing below a winged disk. He wears a long-fringed, short-sleeved cut-away coat made of bands of tufts. A curved panel is cut out of the coat at the front to expose the left leg to the knee. Standing barefoot on mountains the man grasps the trunk of a palm tree. This relief, which is carved in a Northern Syrian Style, is notable for the unusual placement of a lily on a long stalk, which appears to be rising from the man's belt. This depiction finds close parallels in a stone relief from the Late Hittite Palace at Sakçe Gözü (southern Turkey, late eighth century BC), possibly identifying the location of the ivory workshop where this and similar panels from Nimrud were created.

LION'S HEAD

Ivory
9th–8th century BC, Neo-Assyrian
Provenance uncertain
H: 6 cm; W: 6.5 cm; Th: 7 cm
ROM 996.86.1

This head of a male lion, modelled in the round, represents a
piece of ivory sculpture of exceptional, highly dynamic quality.
With its mouth open, exposing its canines and tongue, a
tenseness that is visible in every facial muscle suggests a readiness
to attack. Its original function is difficult to ascertain (the
fixture in the back is a modern add-on) but it seems possible
that it was the finial of a chair's arm rest. The origins and date
of this piece remain uncertain. The facial features of this lion
bear a striking resemblance to those of colossal lion sculptures
from the Ninurta Temple at Nimrud, dating to the ninth
century BC. Lion sculptures (mostly double lions), however,
are also attested at Late Hittite/Aramaic sites such as Tell
Tayinat, Zinçirli, and Sakçe Gözü, which are known to have

THE DYING LION

Gypsum
c. 645–640 BC
From Nineveh, North Palace
H: 16.5 cm; W: 30.6 cm; D: 2.5 cm
BM 1992,0404.1

Since its discovery at Nineveh in the 1850s, this lion has been generally acclaimed as a masterpiece of ancient art. It was originally part of a larger relief panel on which King Ashurbanipal was shown hunting lions in his chariot. This lion is depicted at a slightly smaller scale than those in most lion hunt scenes but without any loss of detail. The sculptor has portrayed the lion's suffering in its last moments of life with great realism and attention to detail. An arrow has fatally wounded the lion, and blood is gushing out of its mouth as it struggles to remain upright. The pronounced veins in the face and dulled eyes are faithful depictions of the lion's pain and suffering. However, the scene was not intended to evoke pity— the killing of a lion was a cause for celebration and a reflection of the prowess of the king.

THE EPIC OF GILGAMESH, TABLET VI

Clay
7th century BC
From Nineveh, library of Ashurbanipal
H: 13 cm; W: 14 cm; D: 2.5 cm
BM K.231

The Epic of Gilgamesh, king of Uruk, is one of the great compositions of world literature. It tells a universal story of one man's heroic quest for immortality, and through the narrative of his journey, deals with issues of life and death which concern us all.

This episode of the epic occurs just after Gilgamesh and Enkidu have killed Humbaba, the monstrous guardian of the cedar forest. Gilgamesh returns to Uruk and cleans himself up. The goddess Ishtar then sees how handsome he is and proposes marriage. Gilgamesh rejects her and reminds her of the terrible fates that she inflicted on her former lovers. Ishtar is enraged and asks her father, the god Anu, for the fiery Bull of Heaven (Taurus).

Gilgamesh and Enkidu kill the Bull of Heaven and while Ishtar mourns the death of the bull, they celebrate their victory

HAMMURAPI STELA (MODERN CAST)

1754 BC or later (original)
Found at Susa (originally from Babylon or Sippar?)
H: 225 cm
B1999 (Penn Cast)

The inscription covering this monument, a stone monolith made of black basalt, contains the most complete version of the so-called Hammurapi law code. Historical events mentioned in the text's prologue indicate that this monument could not have been commissioned before Hammurapi's year 39 (1754 BC), though older versions of the text are attested. The prologue relates how, following Marduk's ascent from city god of Babylon to supreme god, Hammurapi was selected to establish justice among mankind "… so that the strong one may not harm the weak one." The law code itself is composed of 282 court decisions that often encompass very different legal traditions. Retaliatory rulings ("eye for eye, tooth for tooth") find very close parallels in Biblical laws and may be associated with a western Semitic, Amorite tradition. Other laws seek monetary compensations for inflicted damage.

A display panel at the front top of the stela shows Shamash, the sun god, sitting on a throne and handing over the royal insignia (a staff and a ring, probably a roll of string) to Hammurapi, who is facing the god and holding up his hand in a prayer.

HEAD OF A RULER

H.: 10.2 ; W: 6.4 cm
2112–2004 BC or later, Ur III
From Adab (modern Bismaya)
OIM A 173

This head of a bearded male is one of the finest pieces of sculpture from Mesopotamia from the late third millennium BC. The head's facial features—the arched nose and delicate mouth—are finely carved, and betray a striking sensitivity, similar to features of the famous bronze head from Nineveh (pg. 56). The inlays for the eyes are made of ivory and bitumen, mounted in modern blue paste. He wears a broad-rimmed, rounded turban similar, but not identical to, a ruler's cap from the Ur III period. The identity of the person portrayed is uncertain, but both facial modelling and headgear suggest a ruler, possibly of Amorite origin.

STELA OF ASHURBANIPAL

Pink marble
668-655 BC
From Babylon, Esagil temple
H: 36.8 cm; W: 22.2 cm; D: 10.2 cm
BM 90864

On this monument, the Assyrian king Ashurbanipal is shown
as a builder carrying a basket on his head. This was an image
of great antiquity that represented an ideal of kingship in
southern Mesopotamia from the time of the Sumerian kings
(as is shown by the foundation figurine on page 15). Like his
father Esarhaddon, Ashurbanipal carried out a major program of
restoration at Babylon to make up for the sacrilegious destruction
of the holy city by his grandfather Sennacherib. The text records
his good works within the city including the restoration of
a shrine to the god Ea in Esagil, the most important temple
in Babylon dedicated to Marduk the god of the city. He also
mentions his brother who later rebelled against him.

*…I appointed Shamash-shuma-ukin my favourite brother, to
the kingship of Babylon. I completed the work on Esagil which my
father had not finished. I roofed it with immense beams of cedar…*

THE CREATION OF THE WORLD

Clay
6th century BC
From south Iraq
H: 11.5 cm; W: 8.8 cm; D: 3.2 cm
BM 93016

This is the fourth tablet of seven comprising the long epic poem *Enuma Elish*, When on High, one of the most famous accounts of the creation of the world. It tells of the struggle against chaos and the birth of mankind who were created from divine blood and clay in order to serve the gods.

At Babylon the epic was recited on the fourth day of the New Year festival and had special significance as it explained the elevation of the god Marduk to the highest rank of divinity, and the central position of Babylon in Mesopotamian culture. After Marduk saved the gods from attack by Tiamat the ocean, he reorganized the entire universe with Babylon at the centre of it.

A RECORD OF NEBUCHADNEZZAR'S SUCCESSES

Stone
605–562 BC
From Babylon
H: 56.5 cm; W: 50.2 cm; D: 9.5 cm
BM 129397

This stone monument has a slightly rounded reverse side, imitating the shape of a clay writing tablet. In order to evoke the authority of the past, the inscription deliberately copies the style of the script used on monuments of Hammurapi, Babylon's earlier, most revered king. In the long inscription Nebuchadnezzar describes himself as the favourite of Marduk, the chief god of Babylon, and explains how he rebuilt the city in all its splendour. The list of his achievements includes restoring numerous temples, building the huge walls of Babylon, the Processional Way and the Ishtar Gate, the grandest entrance into the city. Nebuchadnezzar was intent on ensuring that his city would last. His buildings were of high-quality mud bricks, baked and also glazed. Unfortunately this ultimately contributed to the destruction of the city's remains as the bricks were later quarried from Babylon for re-use.

STRIDING LION (TERRACOTTA RELIEF)

Baked clay (terracotta), glazed
c. 580 BC, Neo-Babylonian
From Babylon, Southern Citadel
H: 122 cm; W: 183 cm; Th: 8cm
ROM 937.14.1

This relief was one of several depictions of a striding lion
that originally adorned the façade of the palace (the so-called
"Southern Citadel") of King Nebuchadnezzar II (604–562 BC)
at Babylon. Made of moulded bricks that were both painted
and glazed, they were made by the same technique as the rows
of striding bulls and snake dragons that famously adorned the
nearby Ishtar Gate and its Procession Street. Since the reliefs
were assembled in place, the position of each brick had to
be planned ahead carefully. Each brick had to be fired before
applying paint—black for outlines, white for the body, ochre
for the mane, blue for the background—and subsequently be
re-fired for glazing.

As the king of the wild, the lion, in addition to being the
symbol of the goddess Ishtar, was the natural antithesis to the
king, who represented and defended the established order of
civilization.

STELE OF NABONIDUS

Basalt
556–539 BC
From Babylon
H: 58 cm; W: 46 cm; T: 25 cm
BM 90837

This important monument from Babylon shows Nabonidus
under the protection of the symbols of the sun god Shamash,
the goddess Ishtar and, most prominently, the moon god Sin.
Nabonidus was a devotee of the moon god and ultimately
this resulted in much antagonism towards him. As the king of
Babylon, he was expected to worship Marduk above all other
gods. Nabonidus is wearing a Neo-Babylonian-style crown and
a fringed garment. In his left hand he holds a ringed staff or
standard. The symbol it supported is now broken, but its outline
resembles a small crescent moon. A long royal inscription has
been deliberately erased without damaging the adjacent relief
carvings. It is probable that this was done after the Persian
conquest in 539 BC by a military unit instructed by the Persian
king Cyrus to remove the name of the previous king wherever it
was on public display.

MESOPOTAMIA: BACKGROUND AND HISTORY

by Clemens Reichel

From the time of the earliest human settlements in the Fertile Crescent to the rise of world empires that conquered and controlled much of the known world, Mesopotamian history contains many fascinating chapters. Around 7000 BC, it saw the formation of the first villages, the domestication of plants and animals, the so-called Agricultural Revolution. Around 3500 BC, the first cities with gigantic palaces and vast temple complexes emerged, bureaucratic systems evolved, and writing was invented. By 2300 BC, these cities had become part of the first large empire controlled by rulers who were as charismatic as they were ruthless. Mesopotamian history, however, is also a story of inventions and innovations, of human ingenuity in the face of numerous challenges, in an often hostile environment. Many stories could be told, and there are numerous ways of telling them.

This discussion is organized in both chronological as well as topical terms with each chapter representing a time period, in which specific topics, inventions or achievements are highlighted. By primarily focusing on the ROM's own Mesopotamian artifact collection for illustrations, we hope that this guide will be of lasting value beyond the exhibit period of *Mesopotamia: Inventing Our World*.

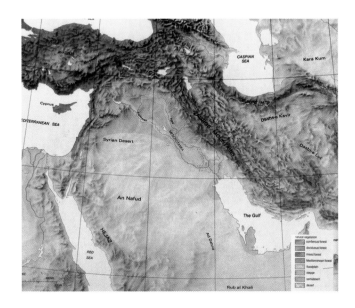

Map of Mesopotamia, showing major vegetation zones.

THE LANDSCAPE

The word "Mesopotamia" is derived from Greek Μεσοποταμία, meaning "(Land) between the Rivers"—the Tigris to the east and Euphrates to the west. The Arabic term for this area—*Jazirah*, meaning "island"— expresses a similar idea of a region that is surrounded by water courses. Geographically, Mesopotamia is comprised of parts of present-day Iraq, eastern Syria, and southeastern Turkey. Culturally and historically, however, Mesopotamian cultures are also found in areas east of the Tigris along the foothills of the Zagros Mountains and in parts of Khuzestan, Iran's southwestern province.

Geography and Climate

Mesopotamia extents over four geographical zones with distinct environmental settings: from the snow-covered peaks of the northern mountains to the desert sands of the south, with rainfall decreasing significantly from north to south. These zones are little changed from ancient times.

• Mountains: The Kurdish mountains of northern Iraq and southeastern Turkey have dry summers and cold, wet winters. Some mountain peaks in this area remain snow-covered all year around. The mountain vegetation includes coniferous (pine, cedar, juniper) and deciduous (oak) trees.

• Foothills: The foothills extend along the southern slopes of the Taurus Mountains in Turkey and the northern Zagros Mountains in Iraq. This area has hot, dry summers and mild, wet winters. Covered by open forests (oak, pine, terebinth) and wild grasses, this area is often called the "Fertile Crescent," where many of the earliest human settlements in the Middle East were located.

• Steppe: The area to the south of the foothills has hot, dry summers and mild, dry winters with minimal rainfall. The vegetation in this area largely consists of open grassland with few, if any, trees.

• Desert: Extending all the way from southern Iraq into the Arabian Peninsula, the desert experiences very hot summers and mild winters. Vegetation is largely absent.

The Tigris and Euphrates rivers and their tributaries flow through these four zones, forming a drainage basin that extends from the mountains of central Turkey and western Iran to the Persian Gulf. This vast watershed creates a well-watered river oasis (p. 39), with rich grasslands and river forests that are home to a diverse fauna. Close to the Persian Gulf, the rivers meander through a marsh landscape with large lakes that are covered extensively with reed. The spring snowmelt in the mountains produces annual flooding, with the rushing rivers carrying off large amounts of silt and clay. Once the rivers leave

River oasis:
Euphrates valley
in northern Syria.

the mountains of Anatolia (south-eastern Turkey) and Syria, the low gradient of the Mesopotamian plain reduces their velocity severely, and most sediments drop out. Much of the landscape that encompasses southern Mesopotamia's lowlands consists of thick sediment layers that were deposited over many millennia.

Annual floods, however, have another kind of fall-out. Eventually, the river beds silt up from continued sedimentation, leading to overland flooding, and rivers carve out new courses. Catastrophic floods are known to have occurred throughout Mesopotamia's history and are reflected in Babylonian epics as well as the biblical Flood story.

Natural Resources

The availability of water played a key role in the development of human habitation. While the alluvial soils of southern Mesopotamia are fertile, annual rainfall rates of less than 200 mm per year do not allow for rain-fed agriculture. Irrigation can offset such adverse preconditions and allow for agricultural yields that are substantially higher than those achieved by relying on natural precipitation. In the past, the people of southern Mesopotamia turned the area into a bread basket that supported a large population by building an array of irrigation canals (see p. 48 for further discussion).

Irrigation agriculture does, however, have inherent dangers.

It must be managed properly. When there is over-irrigation, insufficient drainage, and failure to practise fallowing, the minerals in the river waters—especially salts—build up in the soil, ultimately leading to declining agricultural fertility.

River sediments are rich in clay, so people in ancient times constructed most buildings using unbaked, sun-dried bricks. These bricks were made of mud mixed with straw, which was then poured into wooden moulds. Since fuel (wood, charcoal) was expensive, most bricks remained unbaked. The use of unbaked bricks for construction continues even in modern times. Fire-baked bricks were used predominantly in pavements or wall foundations that needed to be waterproof.

Reed, which grows abundantly in the southern marshes, was another essential building material. Woven into mats, it was used widely for roofing and flooring. In the marshes, reed huts remained the main building type until recently. Stone and wood are absent from southern Mesopotamia. Such materials had to be imported, sometimes over long distances, and hence were rarely used for building.

In southern Mesopotamia, the rivers and canals also served as major traffic arteries, making the transport of bulk in boats over long distances more affordable. Traditional boats were made of reeds or of wooden frames covered with tanned animal hides, often caulked with bitumen.

As much as the rivers shaped the life and times of Mesopotamia, so did the desert sands (p. 7). The "river oasis" is subject to sweeping sand storms that can move vast amounts of sand over large distances. Migrating sand dunes can cover large stretches of agricultural land and settlements for decades if not centuries.

THE REDISCOVERY OF MESOPOTAMIA

Until the nineteenth century, very little was known about the world of ancient Mesopotamia that did not originate from Biblical or Greek sources. That changed in the early 1800s when Europeans took an interest in the area (then part of the Ottoman Empire) out of strategic consideration: easy access to colonies and markets in South and East Asia. Some of the early explorers were British and French diplomats, who spent their leisure time exploring mysterious sand-covered mounds that dotted the Mesopotamian landscape. These were soon recognized as the remains of ancient cities.

In 1811, Claudius Rich, a British businessman and traveller, undertook and subsequently published a first survey of the site of Babylon. For the next few decades, however, the focus of archaeological work in Mesopotamia rested on Assyria. In 1843–1844, Paul Émile Botta (1802–1870), who was appointed

Black Obelisk (19th century copy); of Shalmaneser III, 858–832 BC; inscription mentions King Jehu–the earliest non-Biblical reference in Mesopotamia to an Israelite king; ROM L971.17.A.

French consul to the city of Mosul in northern Iraq, undertook excavations at a village named Khorsabad, discovering a palace of King Sargon II (721–705 BC) (p. 65). Shortly thereafter, a British adventurer, Austen Henry Layard (1817–1894), started excavating at the sites of Nimrud and Nineveh. Many of the wall reliefs and mighty bull figures were removed and transported to the Louvre and the British Museum. Books published about these finds were eagerly received and widely read by the public. Popular exhibits of Ancient Near Eastern Art, such as the Assyrian Pavilion in the Crystal Palace in London (opened in 1866), attracted and fascinated large audiences. Replicas of Assyrian relics such as the famous Black of Obelisk of Nimrud, monumental artifacts, and jewellery remained in great demand throughout much of nineteenth-century Europe (p. 41).

With Europe's appetite for Mesopotamian artifacts increasing, more expeditions were dispatched. Since these excavations were primarily geared to acquiring museum artifacts, they were conducted in unsystematic fashion with very little documentation. Layard's former assistant, Hormuzd Rassam (1826–1910), for example, undertook further excavations for the British Museum in Assyria, but also on Babylonian sites in southern Iraq (Ur, Sippar, Girsu). One of his major accomplishments was the recovery of Ashurbanipal's library at Nineveh, which contained numerous famous cuneiform texts, including the Epic of Gilgamesh (p. 28).

French excavations at the site of Telloh (ancient Girsu), the capital of the state of Lagash in southern Mesopotamia, were undertaken by Ernest de Sarzec from 1877–1900 and resulted in the discovery of numerous statues of Gudea of Lagash (pp. 21, 59), a city ruler dating to 2150 BC, and the discovery of many documents inscribed in the Sumerian language. Excavations between 1889 and 1900 at Nippur, the holy site of the Sumerians, carried out by the University of Pennsylvania and the Babylonian Exploration Fund, not only resulted in the discoveries of many Sumerian epics and mythological texts, but also signalled the arrival of American archaeologists in the Middle East.

A more systematic approach to excavations was introduced by German archaeologists. With most of them trained as architects, they focused on comprehensive architectural exposures. Between 1899 and 1917, Robert Koldewey (1855–1925) excavated Babylon. Principal monuments, such as the glazed-brick decorations from the Ishtar Gate and the Great Procession Street, were shipped to Berlin and painstakingly restored for subsequent display at the Pergamon Museum. From 1900 to 1913, at the site of Assyria's ancient capital Ashur, Walter Andrae developed the technique of excavating walls made of mudbrick, the predominant building material in Mesopotamia.

Following the defeat of the Ottoman Empire after the First World War (1914–1918), the Middle East was divided into British and French mandate zones. Most of Mesopotamia became part of Iraq, but British influence on this newly formed state remained strong, best epitomized in the person of Gertrude Bell (1868–1926). Trained at Oxford and well travelled in the Middle East, Bell was instrumental in drafting Iraq's Antiquities Law, which regulated the issue of excavation permits and the division of finds between the expedition and Iraq's Antiquity Authorities, and in the foundation of the first Iraq Museum.

The 1920s saw the return of British, French, German, and American archaeological teams to Iraq. A joint expedition by the British Museum and the University of Pennsylvania Museum in Philadelphia, under the directorship of Charles Leonard Woolley, excavated the ancient city of Ur, uncovering an ancient cemetery with numerous "royal" graves that were lavishly furnished with artifacts made of gold and precious stones. Well-funded, large-scale excavations by the University of Chicago's Oriental Institute on several sites in the Diyala Region, to the northeast of Baghdad, established for the first time a systematic archaeological sequence for Mesopotamia's early history—the time during which the first cities and states emerged and writing was invented (3200–1800 BC).

From 1928 onwards, German excavations at the site of Uruk exposed majestic temples and public buildings in southern Mesopotamia's earliest city, tracing the origins of the Sumerian culture back into prehistoric periods, while excavations undertaken by Max Mallowan (husband of novelist Agatha Christie) in Arpachiyah in northern Iraq traced Mesopotamia's early village cultures back into the sixth millennium BC—the so-called Halafian culture.

Archaeological work in Iraq following the Second World War saw numerous changes that reflected new approaches towards archaeological work elsewhere. While excavations were resumed on well established sites such as Nimrud and Nippur, new projects at sites such as Jarmo in Kurdistan (northern Iraq) investigated the origins of agriculture and the domestication of animals. The collection of scientific samples (e.g., bones, seeds) to study the ancient environment and palaeozoology of sites became standard procedure during excavations. Numerous surveys undertaken in northern and southern Iraq created systematic inventories of archaeological sites. Offsite work on ancient canals, river courses, and road networks introduced a regional, landscape-based dimension to the settlement archaeology.

The 1960s also saw a tightening of antiquities law, ending the division of archaeological finds. The construction

The Diyala expedition from the University of Chicago's Oriental Institute at Tell Asmar, 1933. Second person from right is James Henry Breasted (late former Director of the Oriental Institute).

T. Cuyler Young (late former Director, Royal Ontario Museum) at Godin Tepe, c. 1973.

of dams along the major rivers and their tributaries resulted in the flooding of numerous archaeological sites, dramatically increasing the need for salvage archaeology. The roster of foreign archaeologists has since been augmented by a growing number of Iraqi scholars, trained abroad as well as at Iraqi universities.

IN THE BEGINNING: NEOLITHIC ORIGINS (10,000–6000 BC)

The earliest traces of human habitations in the Middle East were found in the area of the Fertile Crescent (p. 38). Paleolithic rock caves (15,000–11,000 BC) and temporary shelters were found in the Levant, the Syrian coastal mountains, and the Zagros foothills. The interval between 9000 and 6500 BC, called the "Pre-Pottery Neolithic" period (PPN), saw the start of the Agricultural Revolution with selective growing and hybridization of wild grasses (forerunners to modern-day wheat and barley) and domestication of animals (sheep, goats, pigs, cattle, cats, dogs). Early settlements, found in the Levant, in the Jordan Valley (Jericho), and along the Syrian Euphrates valley, were mostly small, with the largest ones extending over several hectares.

Working of native copper is attested in Anatolia around 8000 BC, where pottery made its first appearance after 7000 BC. During this time, villages continued to grow and showed evidence of centralized storage.

Within Mesopotamia, evidence of early human habitation remains sketchy. Along the foothills of the Zagros, the excavation of the early agricultural village of Jarmo (c. 7500–7000 BC) within Iraq indicated a gradual introduction of pottery. The site of Hassuna, a village west of the Tigris, showed a gradual change in housing structures from makeshift shelters to multi-room buildings (6500–6300 BC). During the Samarran period (6300–6000 BC), houses developed into large multi-room complexes. To the south of Samarra, a first walled settlement was excavated at Tell es-Sawwan.

While pottery continued to be handmade, the number of shapes and the level of sophistication in its decoration increased. Pottery from the later part of the Halaf period (6000–5000 BC), a culture from northern Syria and northern Mesopotamia that spread as far as the Mediterranean, featured multi-coloured ("polychrome") designs that belong to the finest pottery tradition found in the Middle East.

YEARS BC	PERIODS — SOCIAL / TECHNOLOGICAL ACHIEVEMENTS	CULTURES / SITES				
		Levant	Mesopotamia			South
			North			
20,000	**Palaeolithic** • hunters / gatherers • non-sedentary • non-hierarchical family structures	Jericho				
10,000	**Pre-Pottery Neolithic** • adaptation to sedentary lifestyle • introduction of agriculture • domestication of animals		Jarmo			
7,000	**Neolithic** • agricultural village communities • pastoralism (nomadism or semi-nomadism) • specialized craft production • emerging social hierarchies		Hassuna ↓	Samarra ↑ ↓	Halaf ↑ ↓	Ubaid ↑ ↓
4,000				Ubaid		

Table 1. Chronological chart: major time periods and selected cultures / sites for the Neolithic period in Mesopotamia.

Compared to northern Mesopotamia, Syria, and the Levant, our knowledge of early southern Mesopotamia remains very limited. Most of its earliest sites are buried under vast amounts of silt and clay deposited by the rivers of the past millennia. Targeted excavations on a few sites have shown that village communities with large, non-domestic buildings existed as early as 6500 BC in the Southern Mesopotamian alluvium. The recovery of numerous clay sickles on sites, mostly belonging to the later Ubaid culture (5000–4000 BC) highlights the significance of agricultural production. Pottery from this period initially was quite elaborately decorated, but later its decorations were reduced to simple bands or carelessly applied motifs, seemingly due to increased mass production.

The political organization of these early village communities remains poorly understood. Some scholars have interpreted them as chiefdoms; others see elements of "proto-states" present by the Ubaid period.

Cult and Temples

Skulls covered in plaster with eye orbits inlaid with shells, which were found at Jericho and at numerous Pre-Pottery Neolithic sites in Syria, Turkey, and northern Iraq, indicate the presence of ancestral cults as early as 10,000 BC. From about 8000

Clay sickle for agricultural harvesting, surface find at Girsu (southern Iraq); Ubaid period (5000-4000 BC).

BC onwards, "mother-goddesses"—stone or clay figurines that render voluptuously shaped naked women, occasionally in the process of giving birth—appear on sites in northern Mesopotamia, the Levant, and southern Turkey, suggesting the presence of fertility-based cults. Little alabaster figurines of both nude male and female petitioners, found in burials below houses at Tell es-Sawwan, could be early renderings of worshippers in cultic contexts.

In southern Mesopotamia, cultic buildings are attested early on. The earliest of them—found at Eridu, the southernmost of the later cities, and dating to c. 6000 BC—was a single-room shrine with an offering table. Over the next two millennia, this

A reconstruction of the White Temple on a platform at Uruk (c. 3300 BC).

temple was rebuilt repeatedly, evolving into a multi-roomed, tripartite building located on a high terrace. Its outer walls were decorated with niches and buttresses—a hallmark of Mesopotamian religious architecture for millennia to come.

THE RISE OF THE CITY (4000–2300 BC)

The time between 4000 and 3000 BC is associated with many social and technological changes, including the emergence of large cities, the rise of territorial states, and the development of a first writing system. In the past, many scholars have connected these changes with the arrival of a new population group: the Sumerians. Archaeological evidence within Mesopotamia, however, does not support the idea of major migrations.

Pathways to Urban Life

The mechanisms that created the first cities in southern Mesopotamia remain under dispute. In the past, scholars have seen the introduction of irrigation agriculture as a key stimulus. The need to dig and maintain irrigation canals and dikes required large-scale labour organization and craft specialization, leading to the social stratification that transformed a village-based society into an urban society between 4000 and 3000 BC. More recent research, however, suggests that the role of irrigation in this process has been overstated.

Climatological data from 4500–3000 BC suggest that southern Mesopotamia benefitted from monsoonal rainfalls, which may have limited—or even eliminated—any need for irrigation. Rainfall levels might even have been sufficient to sustain pasture land for extensive livestock herds, with the rivers and marshes to the south providing additional protein resources through fish and mammals (wild boars).

Scholars currently consider southern Mesopotamia's position at the head of a large network of waterways—Tigris, Euphrates, and their tributaries—as a key factor that fuelled long-distance trade and urban developments. The rivers provided easy access into Syria, southern Turkey, and western Iran, and bulky items could have been transported on boats or rafts at relatively little

A pile of ration bowls. Bowls like these were used to provide food to large workforces; from Godin Tepe, Iran (3100 BC).

them located on raised terraces, often decorated with niches or elaborate mosaics made of red, white, and black stone or clay cones (p. 48).

Book-keeping and Bureaucrats: The Emergence of Writing

The development of a writing system around 3100 BC remains one of the great hallmarks of this time period. Since most of the texts written before 2000 BC were written in Sumerian, the time between 4000 and 2000 BC has often been called the "Sumerian" Period. This term, however, is misleading. While the Sumerian language was written and presumably spoken in early cities, this does not mean that their inhabitants identified themselves as "Sumerians," nor did they necessarily all speak Sumerian. From about 2500 BC onwards, texts were also written in a Semitic language called "Akkadian" by its speakers. Personal names written on sculptures or in texts were often Semitic in origin, and there is strong indication that members of the ruling elite, even if their names were Sumerian, were actually of Semitic origin. It seems possible that Semitic-speaking groups formed a significant part of Mesopotamia's population, possibly co-existing side-by-side with Sumerians for millennia before writing was invented.

energy expenses. Towards the east, the Persian Gulf opened up trade routes towards the Arabian coast and the Indian subcontinent.

The first cities of Mesopotamia emerged after 4000 BC. The largest one of them was Uruk, which reached a size of 250 hectares by 3100 BC. Excavations show that this city was dominated by large temples and public buildings, some of

DATE	PERIOD		POLITICAL SYSTEM	CULTURAL/TECHNOLOGICAL ACHIEVEMENTS
4000 – 3000 BC	Uruk		"trade empire" headed by city of Uruk	emergence of cities, development of cylinder seals, first writing
3000 – 2900 BC	Jemdet Nasr		decline, probably city states	development of cuneiform writing system
2900 – 2300 BC	Early Dynastic	I	city states	apex of urbanism, large temples, mass production of sculpture (votive figurines)
		II		
		III	emergence of strong political leaders	manufacture of elite products, first historical texts
2300 – 2150 BC	Akkadian		empire, ruled from city of Akkad by kings (some deified)	apex of highly naturalistic monumental art, development of Semitic (Akkadian) writing system
2150 – 2112 BC	Gudea / Lagash II		city state ruled by city governor	development of Neo-Sumerian art (more static, schematic than Akkadian art)
2112 – 2004 BC	Ur III		centralized territorial state, ruled from Ur (some deified)	large temple building projects, highly bureaucratic economic system

Prehistory   History

Table 2. The invention of writing marks the transition between prehistory and history. Writing was invented around 3100 BC, but the earliest historical narratives date to c. 2600 BC.

Early on, human societies in the Middle East developed mechanisms to track expenses and deliveries, and to mark and assert ownership in village-based economies. From at least 6000 BC onwards, storage goods in bags, baskets or jars that were closed up with strings often were "sealed" with a lump of clay. These clay lumps were then marked with impressions from stamps made of stone or bone, often in the shape of animals or body parts, and probably identified families or tribes. They often were perforated, suggesting that they were worn on a string and possibly also served as amulets.

The limited space on stamp seals restricted the design possibilities, which would have been unsuitable for emerging urban bureaucracies in which so much depended on administrative accountability. Cylinder seals, made of limestone, sandstone, bone, or shell, appeared around 3500 BC. They had room for much more nuanced and narrative depictions. Many of the images predominantly show rituals and cultic functions, suggesting that they were used by officials within temple administrations. Frequent displays of herds, often in association with temples, may highlight the economic importance of animal husbandry in temple economies. Seals showing pottery production or weaving—activities often carried out by women—might have been held by the administrators of manufacturing units.

Most early sealings were used to close containers, but door sealings appeared by the late fifth millennium BC. Door-closing mechanisms differed, but in most cases a string attached to the free edge of the door leaf was tied to a peg embedded in the wall next to it. Both peg and string were then wrapped with clay and impressed with a seal. The appearance of door sealings is significant, since their presence indicates that officials specifically oversaw storage—an important step towards a fully bureaucratized society.

Seals and sealings reliably helped to retain control over storable commodities. Numbers were handled differently, through tokens—little counters made of clay, stone or bone in generic shapes (spheres, tetrahedrons) but often reflecting unambiguously figurative items such as animals, animal heads, or jars.

While tokens were practical during transactions, the question of recordong their number afterwards to the satisfaction of both parties must inevitably have arisen, and several solutions appear to have been tried. Excavations at Uruk, Susa, and other Uruk-related sites yielded round, hollow clay balls, dating between 3300–3100 BC, containing groups of tokens that were sealed with cylinder seals (p. 12). These balls served as "envelopes" securing the tokens inside. Marked by a seal of authority, these envelopes could not be broken without it being noticed.

Some envelopes show what appear to be numerical markings on the outside, seemingly addressing the fact that the tokens inside an envelope were invisible. It remains unclear how widespread these notations were, but they do indicate that bureaucratic procedures were about to change. Tokens might still have been useful for counting, but they were no longer needed for recording purposes. Numbers could just as easily be noted through impressions on slabs of clay—the first "proto" tablets (p. 53).

The earliest forms of writing, therefore, appear to have been numerical recordings, along with an indication of what was being counted. Around 3100 BC, these numericals were augmented by first word signs (p. 11). These rendering were principally "logographic" with each sign representing one word or item (e.g., plough, jar, water, bread). These signs, however, could also be combined to create new meanings and pronunciations. A combination of the signs for "head" and "bread," for example, meant "to eat" while "head" and "water" meant "to drink." For several centuries, most writing consisted of accounts and administrative lists, including lexical lists that could be considered early "encyclopediae" of items and of professions.

Writing remained a slow and cumbersome process, since symbols had to be incised into clay with a pointed tool. Around 2900 BC, writing procedures changed dramatically when a new writing tool, a reed stylus that had a triangular cross-section, was introduced. Named "cuneiform" after the wedge-shaped impressions that it created (Latin *cuneus* = "wedge"), this writing system allowed for much faster recording. In order to render images with wedges, however, the images became increasingly abstract. The association with the original picture decreased even more when, due to a change in recording procedures, signs were turned 90 degrees counter-clockwise.

The use of cuneiform writing for Akkadian necessitated significant further abstractions. Like Arabic or Hebrew, Akkadian is an introflective language in which verb forms or cases are formed around verbal "roots." The root of the verb "to cut," for example, is the consonants *prs*. The past tense "he has cut" would be *iprus,* while present/future tense "he cuts / will cut" would be *iparras.* A logographic writing system cannot represent such variations in one sign. Akkadian words, therefore, were rendered syllabically (e.g., *ip-ru-us, i-pa-ra-as*), with each syllable being expressed through one cuneiform sign. Sometimes the reading of a sign in Akkadian was the same as in Sumerian, but quite often secondary syllabic readings were assigned to them.

Just as cuneiform signs and their readings were influenced by their adaptations for Akkadian writing, the Akkadian language itself was influenced. Certain Western Semitic consonants that originally appear to have been in Akkadian were dropped after

Top left:
Group of tokens.

Top right:
Complete clay ball, sealed.

Bottom left:
Clay ball, broken, with tokens inside.

Bottom right:
Simple tablet with numerical markers.

From Choga Mish, southwest Iran, and Hamoukar, northern Syria (3500-3000 BC).

2000 BC since they could not be unambiguously expressed through cuneiform writing.

City States at War

The period between 2900 and 2300 BC, the Early Dynastic time, was tumultuous in Mesopotamia. Historical documents indicate that Mesopotamia was split up into numerous city states during this time, and they were often at war with each other. During this time period, cities in southern Mesopotamia reached unprecedented sizes. In cities such as Uruk, which had grown to more than 400 hectares, agricultural land to feed its large populations must have been in short supply

A long lasting conflict between the states of Lagash and Umma is recorded on the so-called "Vulture Stela" from Girsu, Lagash's capital city. Following repeated provocations by Umma—incursions into Lagash's fertile borderlands and attempts to cut off its water supply—Lagash's ruler Eannatum led his troops into a successful battle against Umma. Text and images on the stela relate the course of the battle in graphic details. One scene shows Eannatum as a larger-than-life figure, holding the defeated enemies as captives within a gigantic net and clubbing them with a mace.

Rise of Kingship

Bureaucracy and conflict march hand-in-hand with politics, and Mesopotamia's concepts of political leadership evolved over time.

During the Uruk period (4000–3000 BC), the ruler seems to have been closely affiliated with the cities' key temples. The famous Warka Vase from Uruk shows the ruler of the city as a provider of the temple of the city goddess Inanna. Iconographic and written evidence allows us to identify this person with a Sumerian title EN—a term that can be translated as "lord" but also "priest." Numerous depictions of this figure with prisoners and, in one case shooting arrows at enemies in front of a burning building, indicate that he is also a political or even military leader.

Most rulers of Early Dynastic city states (2900–2300 BC) held a title commonly translated as "city ruler" or "governor" (Sumerian: ENSÍ). While the term "king" (Sumerian: LUGAL, a ligature of LÚ-GAL, meaning "big man") existed, it most often appeared in the title "King of Kish" (either referring to the city of Kish at the northern edge of the southern alluvial plain, or translating as "King of the Universe"). It is unclear how this title was transferred, and whether any political powers came with it.

Though several palaces have been found in excavations of Early Dynastic cities, they provide relatively little information on how a royal household lived. Most physical evidence of royal households was found among 1800 Early Dynastic and early Akkadian graves at the Royal Cemetery at Ur, where sixteen graves from the later Early Dynastic period have been identified by the excavators as "Royal."

Lavishly furnished with jewellery, weaponry, and royal household items made of gold, silver, and precious stones, the deceased person was joined by large groups of palace personnel—soldiers and palace ladies—ready to serve their king or queen in the afterlife. Some of Mesopotamia's most famous artifacts—such as the gold helmet of Meskalamdug, the Standard of Ur, and the two Rams (p. 19)—were found in the cemetery at Ur, testifying to the enormous wealth of the royal courts. The raw materials were obtained via elaborate, long-distance trade networks: lapis lazuli was imported from northern Afghanistan, while carnelian originated in the Indus valley. Chlorite, the material of which many of the elaborate stone vessels were made, is found in the central Iranian highlands.

Early Dynastic Temples and Religion

From earliest times, temples played an important role in Mesopotamian cities. Temple officials administered large land-holdings and controlled associated manufacturing. Thus, not only did the temples provide places for worship and cultic performances, but also the temple officials were key economic players. For the Early Dynastic period we have rich artifact inventories that provide vital clues about the nature of religious workshops. Decorative inlays that once adorned these temples display their wealth (p. 14).

The layout of Early Dynastic temples was very different from that of their predecessors. The element of openness and

Temple inventory: votive figure, male; fragment of stone bowl with dedicatory inscription by a woman to the goddess Inanna; from Nippur (c. 2500 BC). ROM 950.147, ROM 962.143.27.

Seal of scribe Adda, showing Mesopotamian gods (Ninurta, Ishtar, Shamash, Enki, Isimu) either at sunrise or sunset; from Ur, date: Akkadian (2200 BC); British Museum, BM 89115.

transparency of the Uruk temples, achieved through large numbers of doorways, was replaced by enclosure walls with highly restricted access. A new type of monumental temple, the Temple Oval, dominated Mesopotamian cities (such as the Oval at Tell el-Ubaid). Early Dynastic cities also had numerous small neighbourhood temples and shrines, suggesting the popularization of some cultic functions (see Table 3) that previously might have happened only in large cultic centres.

The artifact assemblages from these temples are dominated by votive figures, statues or statuettes of males or females with their hands folded in attentive or petitioning postures (pp. 13, 16). It seems likely that they served as permanent "stand-ins" before a god on behalf of those whom they represented. These figures, therefore, provide unique insights not only into cultic practices, but also into the social composition of early Mesopotamian cities.

Mesopotamia's pantheon was polytheistic. Every city had a city god who generally performed a specific function. Some other gods appear to have emerged in the agricultural setting of southern Mesopotamia. Their realms included sciences (e.g., medicine) and technology (e.g., irrigation), but also represented human emotions such as love. Astral deities, representing the sun, planets, stars or star constellations, form a separate group that originally might have been associated with groups of nomadic origin.

Many gods or goddesses started as patron deities of a city and fulfilled multiple functions. The formation of city states and first empires led to an increasingly canonized divine pantheon, in which family relations were established and functions were defined.

THE FIRST EMPIRES (2300–1000 BC)

During the latter part of the third millennium BC, new regimes changed the political landscape of Mesopotamia forever. Powerful rulers unified the former city states of Sumer. At times their political control reached far beyond the core region of Mesopotamia, first in the Akkadian Empire and later on in the Neo-Sumerian Ur III state. These early attempts to unify Mesopotamia did not last. The political landscape, however, was to be changed once and forever with the rise of Babylon, which ultimately unified southern Mesopotamia.

Kings and Gods: The Akkadian Empire (2300–2150 BC)

Around 2300 BC, Lugalzagesi, a ruler of Umma, managed to unify southern Mesopotamia by conquering most of the city states. He was soon defeated, however, by a northern ruler named Sharrukin (more commonly rendered as "Sargon" in the Greek form) from Akkade, a city in the northern part of the alluvial plain. (Excavations have so far not discovered this city.) While Sargon's origins remain shrouded in mystery, through later legends, the meaning of his name in Akkadian (šarru(m) kīn = "the king is legitimate") clearly indicates that he needed to affirm the claim to his throne.

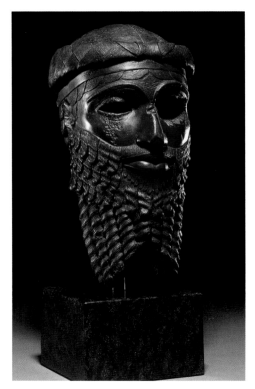

Head of an Akkadian king— either Sargon or Naramsin. Originally part of a statue, it was mutilated at a later date; British Museum replica in copper of the bronze cast from the Iraq Museum from Nineveh (2300–2200 BC); BM 11331.

SUMERIAN NAME	AKKADIAN NAME	GENDER	FUNCTION	HOME TOWN	ANIMAL / EMBLEM	ASTRAL SYMBOL
An	Anu(m)	male	heaven, father of gods	Uruk		
Enlil	Ellil, Bel	male	wind, supreme leader of gods	Nippur	horn crown	
Inanna	Ishtar	female	goddess of love, war	Uruk	lion	Venus
Utu	Shamash	male	sun god, god of justice	Sippar, Larsa	saw, sun rays coming out of shoulder	Sun
Nanna	Sin	male	moon god	Ur	moon crescent	Moon
Enki	Ea	male	lord of ground water ocean (Apsum), wisdom	Eridu	water streams coming out of shoulder, goat fish	
Nininsina	Gula	female	healing, medicine	Isin	dog	
Amar-Utu(k)	Marduk	male		Babylon	snake dragon (mushhushshu)	
Ningirsu, Ninurta	Ninurta, Nimurta	male	warrior god	Girsu, Nippur	bow, double-headed lion mace	
Isimu	Uzmu, Usmu	male	vizier to Enki, Ea		two faces	

Table 3. Examples of Mesopotamian gods.

Sargon founded a dynasty that, for 150 years, controlled most of Mesopotamia (c. 2300–2150 BC). Akkadian became the official language of the state, replacing Sumerian as the language of royal inscriptions. Artwork dating to the Akkadian period, both large (stelae, sculpture) and small (seals), reached an unprecedented level of naturalism and dynamics in the depictions of humans as well as landscapes (p. 54).

Compared to their Sumerian predecessors, Akkadian kings showed very different concepts of kingship in their royal titles, such as "King of the Universe" and "King of the Four World Quarters." Such a view is reflected not only in royal inscriptions (which rell of campaigns into Syria and even southern Anatolia in a quest to secure vital trade-routes) but also in artwork and iconography that displayed proud, confident rulers in monumental sculpture. Sargon's grandson Naramsin took the concept of kingship to a new level by making himself a god. The new concept of a deified ruler is famously displayed in this king's "Victory Stela," found at the site of Susa.

Akkadian kings had to contend with numerous rebellions, especially from the former city states in the south. Later texts connect Akkade's downfall with invasions by groups from the Zagros Mountains, but it is also possible that a failure to effectively break up the structures of the former city states contributed substantially to the empire's demise.

Pious Rulers: Gudea, the Ur III State, and their legacy (2150–1800 BC)

The Akkadian empire was followed by a period generally described as a Sumerian "restoration." Sumerian was once again the language of royal inscriptions, although it is unclear to what degree it continued to be spoken.

The concept and manifestation of rulership changed significantly following the Akkadian period. Sculptures of Gudea, who ruled the city state of Lagash sometime around 2150 BC, picture a pious, devout ruler who submitted to the wishes of principal gods (pp. 21, 60). He undertook extensive building projects, identified through numerous inscriptions buried alongside the foundations.

Southern Mesopotamia was once more unified under Urnammu, the founder of the Third Dynasty of Ur (2112–2004 BC). The centre of political power shifted back to the south, where Ur became the capital of the Ur III State. Although this dynasty ruled for little more than a century, its impact was long-lasting. Extensive building projects in the temples of all major cities of the Sumerian heartland—narrated in numerous building inscriptions—testify to the religious devotion of these kings. Some of their more famous buildings, including the ziqqurats at Ur, Uruk, and Nippur, survived to the present day.

Copy of
seated statue
of Gudea;
original from
Girsu (2150
BC); ROM
955.144.

Even though four of its five rulers were deified during their lifetime, the depiction of Ur III rulers in artwork resembled Gudea more than their Akkadian predecessors. Images on stelae or as foundation figurines show the king as a builder or as bringing offerings to a god.

Incursions of Amorites (Western Semitic tribes), droughts, increased soil salinity, and resulting famines weakened the state, but so did an excessively overblown bureaucratic apparatus that based the economy of the state on centralized redistribution of commodities. By 2004 BC, the Ur III state fell to an invasion from Elam (southwestern Iran), which did away with the last remnants of this Sumerian resurgence.

Following the end of the Ur III state, Mesopotamia reverted to a world of city states, dominated by a rivalry between the cities of Isin and Larsa. Political power during the Isin-Larsa Period (2000-1800 BC) was largely controlled by Amorite (Western Semitic) dynasties. Some concepts of Ur III kingship, such as its divine aspects, survived into this period.

By 1800 BC, Babylon rose from an insignificant settlement to the capital of a dominant state. King Hammurapi (1792–1750 BC) successfully defeated all remaining adversaries and, by 1755 BC, Babylonia controlled all of southern Mesopotamia.

THE RISE OF BABYLON (1800–1500 BC)

Hammurapi's Law Code

Hammurapi was Babylon's most notable king during the Old Babylonian period (1800–1500 BC). One of his lasting achievements was the public establishment of a law collection (often referred to as the "Codex Hammurapi"), the most famous version of which was inscribed on a basalt stela (p. 29). The text is no monolithic creation but rather a collection of established "just verdicts."

The verdicts seem to originate from different traditions. The code's best known section—addressing punishment for the infliction of bodily harm, mostly through retaliatory measures—finds very close parallels in later Biblical laws (e.g., *Exodus* 21:24; *Leviticus* 24:20), suggesting that these traditions were Western Semitic, possibly Amorite, in origin:

§196 If a *citizen* should blind the eye of another *citizen*, they shall blind his eye.

§197 If he should break the bone of another *citizen*, they shall break his bone.

§198 If he should blind the eye of a *commoner* or break the bone of a *commoner*, he shall weigh and deliver 60 shekels of silver.

§199 If he should blind the eye of an *citizen's* slave or break the bone of an *citizen's* slave, he shall weigh and deliver one-half of his value (in silver).

Other laws, such as those governing marriage, on the other hand portray a very different tone. The way in which a husband was to handle his wife's dowry, for example, was regulated in detail. A woman who was divorced by her husband through no fault of her own had to receive her dowry and be supported. Similarly, a woman who had been abandoned by her husband without means of survival was deemed faultless if she "entered the house of another man" to provide for herself, even if she had conceived children as a result of such a relationship.

Babylonian Society

Textual sources from the Old Babylonian and later Kassite period (1500–1150 BC) describe a structured society in which social boundaries were largely impermeable. Legal texts from the Old Babylonian period, such as the Hammurapi law code, identify three classes:

a) Citizens (Akkadian *awīlum*) owned land and house property but also were subject to military service. In the Hammurapi law code, any offence against a citizen incurred the most severe penalties.

b) Commoners (Akkadian *muškēnum*) did not own land

Tablet recording an issue of seed grain. This tablet was found in a clay envelope (front part broken away) that repeated the text and also was sealed for added security (Ur III period; Amar-Suen year 8 = 2039 BC); ROM 910X209.582A+B.

of the few transgressions of slaves addressed by the code was insubordination: a slave who struck the cheek of a citizen would have his ear cut off. The scarcity of offences listed for slaves probably did not indicate mild treatments but, rather, that punishments against them could be inflicted without government sanctions.

In Babylonian society, the family represented the cornerstone of society in both social and economic contexts. The patronymic (name of the father) served as a key identifier for both men and women. Tribal affiliations—references to a common, often mythological, ancestor—were used in pastoral and urban contexts. The concept of a "household" (Sumerian É; Akkadian *bītum*) was modular: a nuclear household could be part of a larger household (such as landholders). The palace (Sumerian É.GAL = "big house") primarily represented the first household of the state.

themselves, though they predominantly (but not exclusively) appear to have worked in agriculture. Offences against a commoner were handled less severely than those against a citizen. c) Slaves (Akkadian *wardum*) were considered property and part of households and, hence, had no independent legal standing, but also had limited liabilities. Hammurapi's law code, for example, provided for sanctions against those harbouring runaway slaves, but not against the slave. One

Economy

Mesopotamian economy was based on both institutional and private entrepreneurship. Numerous manufacturers seem to have been owned or controlled by the crown and by temples, but private activities, especially in trade and manufacture, are clearly attested as well. Most economic exchanges were based on a bartering system in which commodities changed hands without any money involved. The notion of currency, however, was present long before money, as such, was put into circulation.

For most of Mesopotamian history, currency was expressed in silver standards. Although the purchase price was expressed in silver, the actual payments could be made in staple or other commodities, stating the price-relationship between bartered items and silver.

Literacy

In many Babylonian cities, special "schools" were set up to train students in the discipline of writing. These schools could be run privately but could also be operated in association with a temple. Children were trained at an early age in the art of writing. An Old Babylonian literary text from Nippur (c. 1900 BC) provides a detailed insight into the sorrowful life of a school boy:

> …I went to school. In the tablet-house, the monitor said to me: "Why are you late?" I was afraid, my heart beat fast. […] My "school-father" read my tablet to me, (said) "The… is cut off," caned me. […] The teacher in supervising the school duties, looked into house and street in order to pounce upon some one, (said) "Your … is not…," caned me. […] Who was in charge of …(said) "Why when I was not here did

> you talk?" caned me Who was in charge of the… (said) "Why when I was not here did you not keep your head high ? " caned me. Who was in charge of drawing (said) "Why when I was not here did you stand up ? " caned me. Who was in charge of the gate (said) " Why when I was not here did you go out ? " caned me. Who was in charge of the … (said) " Why when I was not here did you take the … ? " caned me. Who was in charge of the Sumerian (said) "You spoke.. ," caned me. …

Taken from Kramer, S.N. 1949: "Schooldays: A Sumerian Composition Relating to the Education of a Scribe," Journal of the American Oriental Society 69:4: 199-215.

Babylon after Hammurapi (1700–1000 BC)

After Hammurapi's death, Babylonia went into a political and economic decline. By 1595 BC, when it was conquered by a Hittite military expedition from Anatolia, it consisted of little more than the area surrounding Babylon. Records from Babylonia for several decades are either scarce or absent.

By 1500 BC, a new population group, the Kassites, gained control of Babylonia. Their origins remain uncertain—it is possible that they immigrated into Babylonia via the highlands of Iran. Just like the Amorites before them, they never formed a major part of the population. For more than 300 years

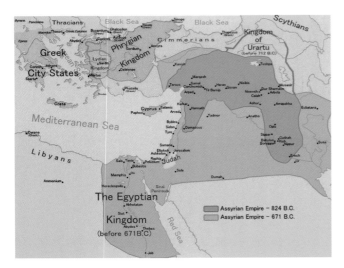

Neo-Assyrian Empire: expansion from the 9th to the 7th century BC.

artwork were shown almost exclusively as symbols, not in human form.

Increased conflicts with Assyria to the north after 1300 BC, and with Elam to the southeast after 1200 BC, weakened the Kassite state. By 1155 BC, it fell victim to an incursion of the Elamite King Shutruk-Nahhunte. This conquest resulted in widespread looting of Mesopotamian temples, during which many famous pieces of art—including the Hammurapi Stela— were carried off to the Elamite capital city of Susa. Although Babylonia was able to rid itself of the Elamite yoke shortly thereafter, the power balance for the next 500 years clearly shifted towards Assyria.

WAR AND POWER: ASSYRIA'S WORLD DOMINATION (1350–612 BC)

Pathway to World Power

For more than a millennium, Assyria was in the shadow of its southern neighbours. Although the city of Ashur, attested from the late third millennium BC, had an important function in interregional trade, networks that extended as far as Anatolia and Central Asia during the Old Assyrian period (2000–1700

(1500–1155 BC), however, they exercised political control over Babylonia from a newly founded capital, Dur Kurigalzu to the southwest of Baghdad. The Kassite period represents a time of stability during which all major sanctuaries in Babylonia were rebuilt. At the same time, artistic expression became highly formalized. Narrative art almost disappeared, while gods in

BC) during the Middle Assyrian period (1350–1000 BC), when Assyria gained control over much of northern Mesopotamia and retained it for more than 200 years. In the west, its power reached the Mediterranean Sea.

Border conflicts with Babylonia escalated, resulting in military incursions and occasional control over Assyria's southern neighbour. Migrations of a new population group, the Arameans, into the heartland of Assyria once more resulted in a temporary decline, but after 900 BC, the beginning of the Neo-Assyrian period, Assyria re-emerged as a regional power.

A sequence of strong kings managed to build an empire that relied heavily on its military machine. Through annual campaigns into neighbouring countries, Assyria not only expanded its territory but also created a string of vassal states from which tributes were extracted. By the late ninth century BC, all of Syria was under Assyrian control, and by 730 BC, Babylonia was once more incorporated into the Assyrian Empire.

Moving through the Levant, the Assyrian kings conquered the state of Israel and famously laid siege to Judah's capital Jerusalem in 702 BC. At the height of this territorial expansion around 680 BC, Assyria's king controlled an empire that extended from western Iran and central Turkey to the Persian Gulf and to southern Egypt.

Capital Cities

With Assyria's expansion to the north and west, the location of Ashur—close to Babylonia—became peripheral. Moreover, the narrow Tigris River valley in this area did not provide enough agricultural land to feed a large population. During the early ninth century BC, Ashurnasirpal II (p. 22) moved the royal residence farther to the north. At Nimrud (ancient name: Kalhu), he built a citadel with palaces and temples and a large, walled, lower town. The king's residence was moved twice more: to Khorsabad (Dur Sharrukin) under Sargon II (721–705 BC) (p. 57) and to Nineveh under Sennacherib (704–682 BC). With an area of seven square kilometres (1,730 acres), Nineveh was the largest city of its time.

Palaces

Much of what we know today about Assyria is based on discoveries in Assyrian palaces. Some of these palaces, which were found on citadel mounds overlooking the city, were the first buildings to be excavated in Mesopotamia. Their discovery shaped subsequent research and much of our present-day understanding of Mesopotamia.

Assyrian palaces were much more than royal residences. They served as "first household" of the state, focal points of

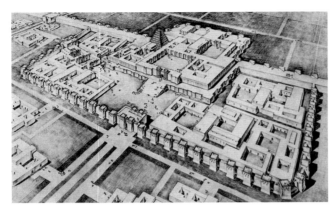

Isometric view of Palace Citadel at Khorsabad; palace of Sargon II (721-705 BC).

government, and locations for state ceremonies, but they were also large economic institutions. The palace entrance was economic in nature, with a courtyard with storage and administrative quarters. The central part of each palace contained the throne room suite, which was elaborately decorated with monumental reliefs and sculptures, and reception suites. The residential part of the palace was generally secluded and accessible to only a selected few.

Assyria's military arsenals were also palatial in size and appearance, and they, too, contained a throne room suite, but for different purposes. Dominated by large courtyards, presumably used for troop reviews, the receipt of foreign dignitaries, and the presentation of tribute, these buildings were located on platforms or mounds along the city walls at a distance from the citadel mounds.

The entrances and most state apartments in Assyrian palaces were decorated with carved reliefs made of limestone, alabaster, or gypsum stone (pp. 23, 25). Their scenes tell visual stories that can be grouped into major themes. Many show cultic performances that involve the king. The royal lion hunt figured prominently in the repertoire of imagery (p. 27). Traces of colour found on numerous reliefs indicate they were originally painted. Others recount military achievements, deportations, and punishment of rebels.

While highlighting the king's achievements, these scenes also convey strong ideological messages. Submitting to Assyria's throne will bring peace and prosperity, while rebellion will result in defeat and annihilation.

Warfare and Deportations

More than any other Mesopotamian power, the Assyrian empire relied on its military might as a principal foundation of the state. Annual military campaigns, glorified in the kings' annals and depicted in great detail in the relief programs, subdued neighbouring states in the north, east, and west, creating a system of tributaries that acted as both a defensive shield and a source of tribute, upon which the Assyrian economy increasingly came to rely.

Core elements of the Assyrian army were its cavalry and its chariotry, which had gained much mobility and speed with the invention of the spoked wheel in the second millennium BC. Rows of archers protected by shield bearers with man-sized shields formed almost invincible and impenetrable walls, both in open combat and during sieges. Most Assyrian soldiers wore helmets and some kind of scale armour. Light infantry soldiers, often wearing little protective gear and using basic weaponry such as sling shots, seem to have been recruited from among foreign mercenaries.

Penalties for subdued enemies, and rebels in particular, could be harsh: they could be flayed, impaled or, if kept alive, blinded. Numerous scenes on Assyrian reliefs show piles of heads, with scribes duly tallying up the number of slain enemies.

During the reign of kings Tiglath-Pileser III (745–727 BC) and Sargon II (721–705 BC), mass deportations of whole populations become common. In most cases, these populations

Assyrian palace relief showing family of deportees, probably from Babylon; from Nineveh, Southwest Palace(?), reign of Sennacherib (704-681 BC); ROM 950.86.

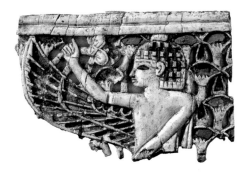

Ivory panel in Egyptianizing style, showing winged male figure in papyrus field; from Nimrud (8th century BC); ROM 961.13.5.

were moved to the Assyrian heartland. Some scholars have suggested that most of the inhabitants of the newly founded Assyrian capitals were deportees. In spite of their forced relocation, deportees were not treated as prisoners: numerous reliefs show whole families, moving their belongings with carts, being led off into exile. Over time most of them— probably including the ten tribes of Israel, deported by Shalmaneser V (727–722 BC) after the fall of Samaria in 722 BC—were assimilated into Assyria's local population.

Tribute and Booty

Following conquest, enemy cities were extensively looted, which is commemorated in royal inscriptions and reliefs. In addition to that, Assyrian vassal states were subjected to regular tribute payments, often in the form of luxury goods.

Some of the most important luxury goods, either received as tribute or gained through conquest, were ivory artifacts (pp. 24, 25, 26). Largely made in western Syria, southern Turkey, and the Levant, most of the items were furniture fittings or decorative bridle harnesses for horses. Stylistically, the decorations on these ivories—which could be geometric or figurative—represent Egyptian, Hittite, Phoenician, and Aramaic traditions, providing clues concerning the locations of ivory production centers. Some ivories decorated in an "Assyrian" style are assumed to have been made locally.

Although thousands of ivory items were found in the palaces of Nimrud and Nineveh, it is unclear how much they were used within Assyria. Most of them were found in storerooms at Fort Shalmaneser, the arsenal of Nimrud. It is possible that these were shown during troop reviews or state visits to highlight the king's power and supremacy over the known world.

Language

By the time the Assyrian empire had reached its apex, it is likely that Aramaic had replaced Assyrian as the *lingua franca* in the empire. As a western Semitic language, Aramaic had an

Barrel-shaped weight with inscription "3 shekel." With a weight of 28 grams, a shekel here would correspond to around 9.3 grams—just slightly more than indicated in Table 4; ROM 931.44.121.

spring floods, which rendered field boundaries invisible. It was likely a result of empirical need rather than the desire to develop a conceptual framework. The development of algebraic equations was impeded by the absence of a way to render "zero" until relatively late (700 BC).

Numerous Mesopotamian standards of measurement are known from textual sources, reflecting volumes, weights, distances, and areal measurements. Early on, standards varied from city to city. Imperial standards were developed during the Akkadian and Ur III period (2300–2000 BC). The relationships between units of measurement were often defined in steps of 6, 10, or 60.

alphabetic writing system (first developed at Ugarit on Syria's west coast around 1300 BC), and hence was written on papyrus instead of clay. The frequent depiction of two Assyrian scribes, one writing on a cuneiform tablet, the other on papyrus, indicates that this linguistic dichotomy was also reflected in the Assyrian imperial administration.

Mathematics and Measurements

Mesopotamian early adaptation of mathematics may have originated from the need to resurvey land plots after annual

1 barleycorn		0.0463 g
1 little shekel	= 3 barleycorns	0.13888 g
1 shekel	= 180 barleycorns = 60 little shekels	8.3333 g
1 mina	= 60 shekels	500 g
1 talent	= 60 minas	30 kg

Table 4. Weight measurements (Akkadian–Ur III; c. 2300–2000 BC).

Clay figurine moulded as a winged spirit holding a bucket (800–700 BC), showing the same motif as the eagle-headed palace relief p. 23; ROM 959.91.39.

Omens

The ancient Mesopotamians believed that divine guidance for critical decisions was issued through omens—visible signs that somehow heralded fateful events. Such signs could include bird flight, natural disasters, planetary constellations, and even dreams, which were collected by professional diviners and recorded in cuneiform texts. These signs, however, were not only sought in natural events. Oracles that could be consulted upon request required a medium for divination, something that was always present and available. Animal organs—in particular sheep livers—were the most common item used for such consultations. Kings employed professional diviners to seek advice before battle. Commoners could seek advice from diviners working at temples. The large herds of sheep that were affiliated with many temples supplied the animals for what must have been one of the most significant functions of an ancient temple.

Spirits and Demons

The world of Mesopotamia was full of spirits, both good and evil, that needed to be appeased or kept away. For an average Mesopotamian, the antagonistic pair of Lamashtu and Pazuzu was of great significance. The demon Lamashtu—frequently depicted on plaques with a hairy body, the head of a lioness, donkey teeth and ears, long fingers and fingernails, and bird's feet—was widely feared. She was the bringer of diseases and commonly was associated with miscarriages and infant deaths. Pazuzu, a winged demon with a lion's or dog's head, bird's feet, and a scorpion's tail, was also an evil demon who brought fever, drought, and famine, but he was considered to be Lamashtu's key adversary and, hence, was invoked frequently.

Some of these demons or monsters, such as the Mushushshu, combined aspects of several animals: a snake, a bird, and an eagle. Others, such as the Lamassu (a human-headed bull figure, usually flanking the entrances of Assyrian palaces) combined anthropomorphic and zoomorphic attributes. A horn crown worn by both of them indicates that they were deities.

Clay figurines of protective spirits were often used in households (p. 69). Buried under the threshold of the house, they could prevent evil spirits such as Lamashtu from entering the premises. Some of these figures were inscribed with instructions or incantations.

Assyria's Final Decade

The Assyrian empire reached its greatest extent under Esarhaddon (680–669 BC), when Egypt was conquered. Following the reign of his son Ashurbanipal (668–c. 627 BC), the empire faced a new alliance between Babylonia and Medea, a powerful political entity located in western Iran. In 614 BC, the capitals of Ashur and Nimrud were conquered by the Medes. Two years later, Nineveh had fallen into the hands of the alliance. By 609 BC, the last remnants of the Assyrian empire were defeated on the Harran Plain in southern Turkey.

Even though it was a powerful entity that survived for centuries through its vastly superior military power, the Assyrian empire ultimately lacked the resilience and cohesion to survive longer periods of political crises and economic weaknesses.

THE WRITING ON THE WALL: BABYLONIAN MYTH AND REALITY (612–539 BC)

Throughout most of the time of the Assyrian supremacy, Babylon's power remained limited. Periods of Assyrian control alternated with times of political independence, which often resulted in punitive actions from Assyria. In southern Babylonia, a new power factor—the Chaldeans—established themselves in an area called the "Sealand" that was controlled by powerful tribes. Starting in 721 BC, one of their leaders, Marduk-Apla-iddina II (known from the Bible as Merodach-Baladan), repeatedly seized control of Babylon from the Assyrians during the reigns of Sargon II (721-705 BC) and Sennacherib (704-681 BC). Sennacherib's response, a complete annihilation of the city of Babylon that was widely commemorated in his inscriptions, was of a temporary nature. Sennacherib's son Esarhaddon (680-669 BC) restored Babylon and returned the statue of Marduk, Babylon's principal god, to its shrine.

By 625 BC, Babylonia under Nabopolassar (625–605 BC) had shaken off Assyrian control. Forming an alliance with the Medes in western Iran, the Assyrian empire was defeated between 614 and 609 BC. For a period of less then 100 years,

A 3-D rendition of the Ishtar Gate.

Babylonia once more re-emerged as the centre of political control and culture in the Ancient Near East. This time frame is associated with many names, monuments, and events known from the Biblical narratives—King Nebuchadnezzar II, the Tower of Babel, and the Babylonian Captivity of the Jews.

By 600 BC, Babylon was the largest city in the world, covering an area of seven square kilometres, with an outer and an inner city that were both walled and protected by moats. The inner city could be entered through a series of gates of which the Ishtar Gate, which was preceded by a monumental procession street, is the most famous. Both the gate and the walls along the streets were decorated with blue-glazed bricks and reliefs, and painted representations of lions, bulls, and snake-dragons (mushhushshu), presenting a striking and awe-inspiring impression. To the west of the Ishtar Gate was the Southern Citadel, a mighty palace built by King Nebuchadnezzar II (605–562 BC). Built as a massive enclosure along the northern edge of the inner city wall, its architecture resembled that of the neighbouring Ishtar Gate and the Great Procession Street. Originally constructed under Nabopolassar but rebuilt by Nebuchadnezzar, the façade of its throne room was decorated with glazed tile reliefs that showed sacred trees and striding lions (p. 34).

A vaulted area in the northeastern section of the citadel had been interpreted by the excavators as the location of Babylon's

"Hanging Gardens." Today, however, most archaeologists interpret this building unit as a storage area.

The Procession Street led on to Esagila, the temple of Marduk, and Etemenanki Temple: "Wall between Heaven and Earth," and the Ziqqurat (temple tower). Forming a square of 91 x 91 metres, and reportedly reaching a height of 91 metres over seven storeys, it dominated Babylon's skyline. Built during the reign of Nebuchadnezzar II at a considerable expense—using vast amounts of baked bricks and using bitumen as mortar—it provided the setting for the "Tower of Babel" story, the biblical allegory that epitomizes a misguided human quest to be equal with God (see *Genesis* 11:1-9).

Although Babylonia did not pursue the politics of colonization beyond the heartland that had been in instituted by the Assyrians, they continued the policies of forced deportations of unruly populations in conquered territories. The most famous example of it is the "Babylonian Captivity," the deportation of the inhabitants of the state of Judah to Babylonia between 597 and 582, which lasted until 538 BC (*Jeremiah* 39-43, *2 Kings, 2 Chronicles, Daniel* 1-6).

Turmoil ensued upon Nebuchadnezzar's death. Following a quick succession of two kings Nabonidus, the son of the governor of Harran (a city close to Urfa in southern Turkey), seized the throne in 555 BC. His family history is as illustrious as his life: his mother Adda-Guppi lived an eventful life to the age of 104. There are strong indications that Nabonidus descended from an Assyrian family. His focus on the cult of the moon god Sin antagonized the Marduk priests at Babylon. Following a rebellion in Babylon, Nabonidus spent ten years of self-imposed exile in the desert oasis of Teima (now in Saudi Arabia), home to a sanctuary for the moon god. During this time, he left state affairs to his son Bel-shar-uṣur, who is rendered in the Bible as "Belshazzar" (and probably confused with his father).

The famous story of the prophet Daniel interpreting a mysterious "Writing on the Wall" to Belshazzar during a feast as a sign of impending doom was a Biblical allegory (*Daniel* 5:25-28), but, Babylon's days were indeed numbered. In 539 BC, it fell into the hands of Cyrus, the king of the newly founded Achaemenid Empire in Persia, after a nine-month siege. Cyrus's statements that the city was neither destroyed nor looted (in fact it was turned into one of the capitals of the Persian Empire) highlight the advent of a new, more liberal, type of political ideology. The Jewish deportees were allowed to return home (hence the generally positive view of Persian overlordship in the Bible).

The fall of Babylon to Cyrus does not mark the end of Mesopotamia's grandeur. As one of the empire's central provinces, Babylonia flourished and, in fact, benefitted from its incorporation into a larger state.

EPILOGUE

Mesopotamia after "Mesopotamia"

Mesopotamian civilization ended neither with the Babylonian nor with the Persian Empire. Following Alexander's victory over Persia's troops in 331 BC, Mesopotamia became part of the Greek world. Following Alexander's death in 323 BC, his general Seleucus founded the Seleucid Empire, a vast state that extended from the Mediterranean to Afghanistan which controlled Mesopotamia until 133 BC. Becoming part of the Parthian (150/130 BC–116 AD, 118–226 AD), Roman (116–118 AD), and Sassanian (226–636 AD) empires, urban centres in Mesopotamia continued to flourish, though their locations shifted and their faces changed significantly. Cuneiform writing was abandoned during the first century AD. Next to Aramaic, Greek had become a widely used language.

By the time of the Arab conquest in 633/636, Christianity had become the dominant religion. With the establishment of Baghdad as capital of the Abbasid Empire in 734 AD, the focus of power once more shifted to Mesopotamia, with its cities remaining centres of science and learning. The Mongol invasion of 1258 resulted in widespread destruction, abandonment of cities, and the collapse of irrigation systems. This was a decisive blow to the region from which it never fully recovered. Following the conquest by the Turkish Empire in 1636, it remained a cultural backwater of the Ottoman Empire until 1918. With the foundation of Iraq in 1920, Mesopotamia was once more united in a state that closely matched the extent of Babylonia and the heartland of Assyria.

The oil boom of the twentieth century turned Iraq into one of the most prosperous nations of the Arab world, with a high standard of living, excellent medical facilities, and a comprehensive education system. In recent decades this development, unfortunately, was halted due to several wars: the Iran-Iraq War (1980–1988) was very costly in human lives and many of the country's resources were redirected to war efforts. Following Iraq's invasion of Kuwait in August 1990, the First Gulf War (January–March 1991) destroyed much of Iraq's infrastructure. Economic embargoes imposed by the West led to widespread impoverishment. The Iraq War of March–April 2003 had even more disastrous consequences: the collapse of all government institutions following a U.S.-led invasion resulted in political instability, an armed resistance, and the outbreak of sectarian violence. Following national elections in 2005 and 2010, the establishment of a civilian government, and the withdrawal of the last U.S. troops in December 2011 conditions improved significantly, but, the security situation in Iraq continues to be tense.

A Threat to Iraq's Cultural Heritage

Iraq's rich archaeological heritage was badly affected by these events. While archaeological fieldwork continued throughout the Iran-Iraq War during the 1980s, an economic embargo imposed after the 1991 Gulf War not only made foreign fieldwork impossible but also caused a widespread economic impoverishment that led to the looting of numerous archaeological sites—a problem that up to that point had basically not existed in Iraq.

Serious as these developments were, they barely measure up to what happened after the 2003 Iraq War: following the fall of Baghdad on April 9, 2003, the Iraq Museum itself was looted for several days. Some 15,000 items were taken from the museum's exhibits and storage rooms, of which 8,000 are still presumed to be missing. Even worse was yet to come: in the absence of any effective police control in Iraq's countryside, major archaeological sites—especially in the south (Sumer, Babylonia)—saw an unprecedented level of looting. Honey-combed by pits and tunnelled to a depth of several metres, many of these sites were irrecoverably destroyed. Over the past two decades Iraqi archaeologists have done their best to curb these lootings. Some of them started rescue excavations to pre-empt the looters' efforts—a difficult and often very dangerous undertaking.

After the fall of Baghdad in April 2003, the Iraq Museum—one of the world's most precious collections—was overrun by looters.

In the past few years, some foreign archaeologists have been returning. Most of them are working in the autonomous region of Kurdistan in the north, which has seen less violence, but a few teams are trying to revive previous excavations or start new projects in the south. Resuming work remains difficult and at times thorny, but there is hope that the lands of Sumer, Assyria, and Babylonia will soon experience a new wave of exploration. Mesopotamia, one of mankind's oldest Cradles of Civilization, still has a lot of secrets to reveal.

ROM CENTRE OF DISCOVERY: ANCIENT CULTURES

ROM Ancient Cultures is an essential destination for learning about the civilizations of the past, understanding how they can inform our lives today, and helping us plan for the future. This Centre of Discovery enhances and reinvigorates the experience of learning and discovery at the ROM, connecting visitors to their world and to each other.

ROM Ancient Cultures engages a broad community—including both professionals and non-specialists—in learning about, discussing, contributing toward, sharing, and finding relevance in the Museum's research and collections. From the evolution of our early human ancestors in China to the technological innovations of Mesopotamia to the global economy of ancient Rome, the ROM's research and collections illustrate the diversity of past human experience.

Research within the Centre seeks to explore the roots of our contemporary world through archaeological fieldwork and the examination and analysis of archaeological objects. Curators of the Centre bring world-recognized expertise in the archaeology, art history, and cultural history of diverse geographical areas. Their research is currently focused on East Asia, the Middle East, North Africa, Europe, and the Andes, and also engages with other regions of the globe. Using a cross-cultural, multidisciplinary approach, ROM Ancient Cultures investigates a number of important research themes:

human origins
diversity of the human experience
technological change and innovation
human complexity and interaction
symbolism, belief, and thought
preservation of cultural heritage

ROM Ancient Cultures provides opportunities to learn about and discuss current research and knowledge about past civilizations through conversations, programs, galleries, and exhibits at the Museum, online, and throughout the province. The Museum has twenty-three galleries containing thematic links to the Centre, including The Joey and Toby Tanenbaum Gallery of Rome and the Near East, The Joey and Toby Tanenbaum Gallery of Byzantium, and The A.G. Leventis Foundation Gallery of Ancient Cyprus. We engage diverse audiences, including families, adults, and students.

MESOPOTAMIA LECTURE SERIES

Enthusiasts and experts are invited to attend the Mesopotamia Lecture Series with opportunities to engage in exploration, dialogue, and debate around key issues and current scholarship. The lectures will bring high-profile, internationally known speakers to offer their perspective on themes and issues related to this ancient culture, from disciplines such as archaeology, art history, linguistics, and the history of science.

7-8 p.m.
All talks will be held at the Signy and Cléophée Eaton Theatre *unless otherwise specified.*

> **June 27**
Kings of the Universe: The Rise and Development of Political Leadership in Mesopotamia
Dr. Clemens Reichel
ROM Associate Curator of Ancient Near East

> **September 12**
Lions, Temples and Tablets on the Plain of Antioch: Assyrian Imperialism on the Mesopotamian Periphery
Dr. Timothy Harrison
Professor of Near and Middle Eastern Civilizations, University of Toronto

> **September 26**
New Light on an Administrative Device from the Dawn of Writing in the Ancient Near East
Dr. Christopher Woods
Professor of Near Eastern Languages & Civilizations, University of Chicago

> **October 10**
The Royal Cemetery at Ur
Dr. Richard Zettler
Chair, Near Eastern Languages & Civilizations, University of Pennsylvania; Associate Curator in Charge, Near East, University of Pennsylvania Museum of Archaeology & Anthropology

> **November 7**
Revealing Meaning in the Art of the Ancient Near East
Dr. Irene Winter
Professor Emerita of Fine Arts, Harvard University

> **November 21**
Foresight, Forecasting, and the Future in Ancient Mesopotamia
Dr. Francesca Rothberg
Professor of Near Eastern Studies, University of California, Berkeley

MESSAGES FROM OUR SPONSORS

RSA Insurance Partners with the ROM
to Present *Mesopotamia*

Leading home, auto and business insurer RSA Insurance is partnering with the ROM to present *Mesopotamia*—the ROM's summer blockbuster exhibition. This stunning exhibition showcases more than 170 priceless objects from the celebrated holdings of the British Museum, most of which have never been seen in Canada.

"As a global insurer with a proud heritage supporting progress, people and businesses around the world for over 300 years, we're incredibly excited to be working alongside the ROM to bring these amazing artifacts to life and we are confident this exhibition will prove to be a fascinating adventure for all," says Rowan Saunders, President & CEO, RSA Insurance.

The ROM is hosting *Mesopotamia* in its premiere North American engagement from June 22, 2013 to January 5, 2014. This acclaimed exhibition also features artifacts from the ROM's own renowned collections and from the University of Chicago Oriental Institute Museum, University of Pennsylvania Museum of Archaeology and Anthropology (Penn Museum, Philadelphia) and Detroit Institute of Arts.

As one of Canada and Ontario's largest insurance providers, RSA knows how important it is to recognize the past to plan for what's to come - whether re-building the present or protecting our future. "RSA Insurance is proud to partner with the ROM to make the wonders of ancient Mesopotamia accessible to all in this one-of-a-kind exhibition for Canada and North America," says Saunders.

Mohammad Al Zaibak and Family Generously Support *Mesopotamia* as Lead Exhibit Patron

ROM Trustee Mohammad Al Zaibak has been a strong ROM supporter for the past 13 years. A member of the Royal Patrons Circle since 2008, he has given considerable time and financial support to numerous Museum projects.

"This exhibition will illustrate the incredible developments of an ancient world, revealing how it is still timely and relevant to our modern-day lives," says Al Zaibak. "It gives me great pleasure to help share the rich cultural legacy and heritage that began in what is now Iraq, Syria and Turkey."

Widely considered to be the cradle of civilization, Mesopotamia in Arabic is termed *Jazirah* (island) or Bilad-al-Rafidayn (between between two rivers).

The opening of this highly anticipated exhibition will coincide with the launch of the ROM's new Centre of Discovery for Ancient Cultures. In this Centre, world-class experts and innovative partnerships will ensure dynamic experiential learning for children and adults alike. "ROM Ancient Cultures will serve as a powerful forum for learning, discussion and understanding," says Al Zaibak. "Exhibitions like *Mesopotamia* can help us make sense of past cultures and how they inform our present in a vibrant multicultural society."

Young Patrons Circle Supports *Mesopotamia* as Exhibit Patron

The Young Patrons Circle (YPC) is a unique and personal way to experience the ROM. Young professionals with a passion for natural history and world cultures make an annual philanthropic gift to the Museum and enjoy exclusive access to ROM exhibitions, galleries, curators, vaults and private collections.

Since its launch in 2005, YPC donors have contributed more than $1.4 million to the ROM. This year the group is breaking new ground by generously supporting *Mesopotamia* as the show's Exhibit Patron. "Many of our patrons are interested in ancient cultures and we're looking forward to helping the ROM bring visitors a modern take on Mesopotamia," says YPC Chair Anna-Maria Kaneff.

Interested in learning more about or joining YPC? Email ypc@rom.on.ca or call 416.586.8003. You can also visit rom.on.ca/ypc or follow @YPCROM on Twitter.

MOHAMMAD AL ZAIBAK AND FAMILY

Published by the Royal Ontario Museum with the generous support of the Louise Hawley Stone Charitable Trust. The Stone Trust generates significant annual funding for the Museum, providing a steady stream of support that is used to purchase new acquisitions and to produce publications related to the ROM's collections. The Louise Hawley Stone Charitable Trust was established in 1998 when the ROM received a charitable trust of nearly $50 million—the largest cash bequest ever received by the Museum—by its long-time friend and supporter, the late Louise Hawley Stone (1904–1997).

Royal Ontario Museum | 100 Queen's Park | Toronto, Ontario M5S 2C6
rom.on.ca

Library and Archives Canada Cataloguing in Publication

Reichel, Clemens D., author
    Mesopotamia : inventing our world / Clemens Reichel.

ISBN 978-0-88854-494-0 (pbk.)

    1. Iraq—Antiquities—Exhibitions. 2. Iraq—Civilization—To 634—
Exhibitions. I. Title.

DS69.T67R69 2013   935   C2013-903848-5

La Mesopotamie, ou, L'invention de notre monde.
ISBN 978-0-88854-496-4

Clemens Reichel is Assistant Professor of Mesopotamian Archaeology at the University of Toronto's Department of Near Middle Eastern Civilizations and Associate Curator for Ancient Near Eastern Archaeology, Department of World Cultures, ROM.

Sarah Collins is Curator for Early Mesopotamia, Middle East department, British Museum.

© The Trustees of the British Museum: pp. 11, 12, 13, 14, 15, 17, 18, 22, 23, 24, 27, 28, 31, 32, 33, 35, 56, 57; A. Tayfun Oner: p. 71; Bill Pratt: p. 52; Brian Boyle: pp. 3, 25, 26, 34, 40, 49, 55, 59, 62, 67, 68, 69; Clemens Reichel: pp. 7, 8, 29, 39, 47, 53; Detroit Institute of Arts Museum: p. 21; Ernst Heinrich: Die Tempel und Heiligtümer im alten Mesopotamean. Denkmäler Antiker Architektur 14, 1982. Berlin: De Gruyter: p. 48; Michael Roaf, Cultural Atlas of Mesopotamia (1990), Facts On File, Inc.: p. 37; The Oriental Institute of the University of Chicago: pp. 30, 44, 66; University of Pennsylvania Museum of Archaeology and Anthropology: pp. 16, 19, 20; Wikipedia Commons: p. 63; Yanis Kontos, Polaris Images: p. 74

Cover image: *Foundation tablet* (detail), Steatite, Ur, 2094–2047 BC,
© The Trustees of the British Museum.

Printed and bound in Canada by Transcontinental Interglobe, Beauceville East, Quebec.

The Royal Ontario Museum is an agency of the Government of Ontario.

MIX
Paper from
responsible sources
FSC® C011825
www.fsc.org